Gauguin

For hundreds of years, painters worked mostly in their studios. But, at the end of the nineteenth century, a group of young artists decided to paint outdoors. These artists, called Impressionists, sought the natural light of the sun. They painted using bright cheerful colors. Some of these painters settled away from Paris (the art capital of the world at that time) in southern France, others visited Spain and North Africa. One artist, Paul Gauguin, chose to live far away from his home in France, in a tropical country called Tahiti. In Tahiti he learned how to paint using bright and vibrant colors. His paintings also took on a new style where the shapes of people and things were simplified.

1

Paradise

Notice the golden glow of the sun. The people are tan and they wear light dresses and festive colors. Gauguin wanted his paintings to show the busy people in France that there was another way to live. He painted people who were happy and content but who were not bustling about working and trying to get rich. He wanted society to see that just by being alive, we already have everything we need to be happy.

Femmes de Tahiti (Women of Tahiti) • Musée d'Orsay, Paris.

Freedom, Calm,

In Gauguin's paintings, life is easy for people and animals. He wanted to paint people enjoying life slowly. "I am leaving to be left alone, to be freed from the influence of civilization." He said, "I only want to do simple art, very simple." The play of colors and the calmness of the people give his paintings a feeling of peace and makes us want to dream.

Where Do We Come From? Who Are We? Where Are We Going? • Museum of Fine Arts, Boston.

Gentleness

Gauguin painted inviting rivers and trees filled with fruit. He painted young and old people living in harmony with nature. This is not actually the way it was at the time Gauguin lived in Tahiti, it is the way he dreamed it could be.

Color

Gauguin wanted to combine both old and new art techniques to create beautiful paintings. He wanted to paint images of untouched nature and people who live off of the land in a way no one had before. As a result, his paintings are simplified. The flatness of the images makes viewers focus on the shapes and colors in the paintings. It forces us to look at people in a new way. The colors he uses are strong. Notice how vibrant the red is next to the washed out blue dress—the bold colors are shockingly different from each other. This mix of simple primitive shapes and mixture of brightly colored modern paints, created a wildly exciting and new kind of artwork.

"With elements entirely new and wild, I'm going to do beautiful things... I am dreaming of violent harmonies..." said Gauguin.

This Femme à la fleur (Woman with Flower) is the first portrait painted by Gauguin in Tahiti. More than landscapes or still lifes, it was the people on the island that Gauguin was interested in.

Vahine no te Tiare
Woman with Flower

A red dog... What an idea! The critics of the time were outraged.
Before Gauguin, a painter had never exaggerated his use of colors so much!

AREAREA

To give his paintings a truly exotic flavor, Gauguin not only turned to his imagination, but to the art of other cultures as well. The scene below was inspired by an Egyptian painting dating from the time of Pharaohs. Look at the dignity of the women sitting on the bench, their nobleness! They have the look of goddesses. In Gauguin's time no one cared much about the remote peoples discovered by the explorers; their traditions were ridiculed. But Gauguin observed everything with respect.

Ta Matete • Kunstmuseum, Basel © photo Giraudon.

Horsemen on the Beach • Niarchos Collection, Greece © photo Artephot/Held.

Freedom

Gauguin believed that far from the cities and modernism, happiness was near. Look at these riders without saddles, boots, or fancy riding clothes. Their life seems very simple compared to the life in Paris at the same time. The painter's technique seems simple too.

Gauguin's use of simple shapes, peaceful scenes, and contrasting colors brought a whole new style of art to the painting world—influencing artists for years to come.

Paul Gauguin was born in Paris in 1848. One of his grandmothers was a native of Peru. At the age of seventeen, Paul enlisted in the navy and, for six years, traveled around the world. Then he worked as a bank employee, got married, and became the father of three children.

He earned a good living and became interested in Impressionist painting, which he started collecting. Eventually, for his own pleasure, he too started painting. He was twenty-five. He took some art classes and kept company with artists. Everything seemed to be going his way. But, in 1883, an economic crisis caused him to lose his job. So he decided to make a living with his painting and his real adventure began!

But try as he might to be a painter, he could not sell his paintings. Because he had no money to support his family, his wife and children went to live with her parents. Alone, Gauguin stayed in Brittany, where many other painters lived and worked.